Clovis Crawfish
and the
Orphan Zo-Zo

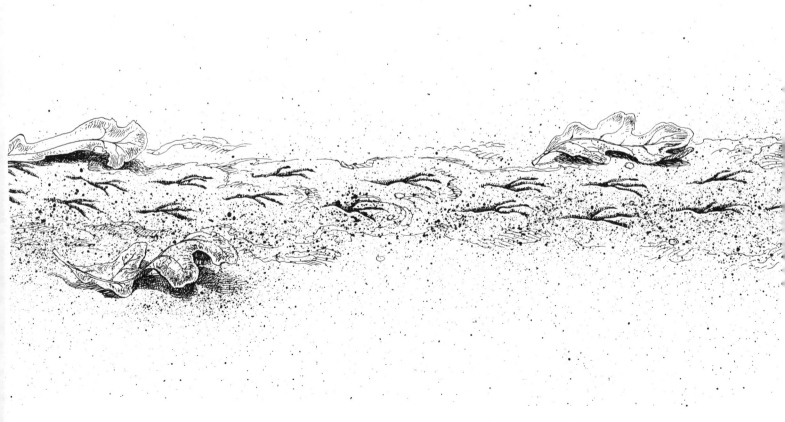

Mary Alice Fontenot

Clovis Crawfish and the Orphan Zo~Zo

Illustrated by Eric Vincent

Pelican Publishing Company
GRETNA 1983

Also in the series by Mary Alice Fontenot
and illustrated by Eric Vincent

Clovis Crawfish and the Singing Cigales

Library of Congress Cataloging in Publication Data

Fontenot, Mary Alice.
  Clovis Crawfish and the orphan Zo-Zo.

  Summary: A group of French-speaking Louisiana bayou
animals save the life of an orphaned baby blue jay.
  [1. Animals—Fiction. 2. Cajuns—Fiction] I. Vincent, Eric, ill. II. Title.
PZ7.F73575Clp   [Fic]   81-17740
ISBN 0-88289-312-2   AACR2

Design and production by Eric Vincent

Manufactured in the United States of America
Published by Pelican Publishing Company, Inc.
1101 Monroe Street, Gretna, Louisiana 70053

For Michael René Dardeau and Vaughan Burdin Baker
Parrain and *Marraine* of *P'tit Zo-Zo*

A flash of lightning zigzagged across the sky. Lizette Lizard hid her eyes.

Thunder rumbled and grumbled. René Rainfrog covered his ears.

Raindrops as big as dewberries spattered off the oak-tree leaves.

The wind blew so hard that Clovis Crawfish's whiskers went up and down and around and around. Clovis backed down into the round hole in the middle of his mud house on the bank of the bayou in south Louisiana.

The wind howled through the treetops and swished the water in the bayou. It blew so hard that pinecones and tree branches came crashing down.

After a while the wind calmed down. A ray of sunshine streaked out from behind the black and blue clouds. The storm was over.

René Rainfrog stuck his head down into the hole in Clovis' mud house.

"*Dépêche-toi*, Clovis!" cried René, which means "Hurry!" in Acadian-French.

Clovis crawled out as fast as he could. René Rainfrog was hopping around on the bayou bank. Lizette Lizard came racing down the mus-cadine vine. Gaston Grasshopper hopped up on top of a round toadstool.

"Look!" croaked René Rainfrog. "It's a *p'tit zo-zo!*"
which is the way Cajun children say "little bird."
   A baby bird was flopping around on the ground, its feathers all wet
and muddy.

Clovis twirled his whiskers and stared at the baby bird flopping around in the mud.

"We can't just let it die," said Clovis. "It's just a baby. Besides, it's not the baby's fault that birds eat bugs. Lots of living things live on other living things. Like Sosthene Snake. If I'm not careful, Sosthene will eat me!"

"It was the storm!" said Clovis Crawfish. "The wind blew it out of its nest!"

"*Pauvre 'tite bête!*" said Lizette Lizard, which means "poor little thing!"

"Will it die?" asked René Rainfrog.

"Yes, it will!" said Clovis Crawfish. "Unless we take care of it and find something for it to eat!"

"But it's a baby blue jay!" mumbled Christophe Cricket.

"And when it grows up it might eat us!" grumbled Gaston Grasshopper.

Clovis twirled his whiskers and stared at the baby bird flopping around in the mud.

"We can't just let it die," said Clovis. "It's just a baby. Besides, it's not the baby's fault that birds eat bugs. Lots of living things live on other living things. Like Sosthene Snake. If I'm not careful, Sosthene will eat me!"

Clovis Crawfish took one look and said, "*Mais jamais!*" which is the way Acadians say "But no!" He flexed his claws and twirled his long whiskers.

"What's it doing down here?" asked Christophe Cricket. "This is no place for a baby bird!"

"Baby birds belong in a nest high up in a tree!" said Gaston Grasshopper. "How did it get down here?"

Christophe Cricket and Gaston Grasshopper went off by themselves mumbling and grumbling.

René Rainfrog and Lizette Lizard hid themselves in the leaves of
the muscadine vine.

"*Arrête!*" cried Clovis, which is the way to say "Stop!" in French.
He snapped his big sharp claws and wiggled his whiskers real fast.

"Come back!" he said. "This poor little orphan bird needs all of us!"

Clovis Crawfish's friends gathered around.

René Rainfrog brought the baby bird a ripe muscadine. Bertile Butterfly brought a sip of nectar in a honeysuckle cup. Lizette Lizard dragged in some Spanish moss to clean the baby's feathers.

Fernand Frog shared some fish eggs and Maurice Mosquito Hawk flew back and forth a hundred and three times to bring mosquitoes for the orphan bird to eat.

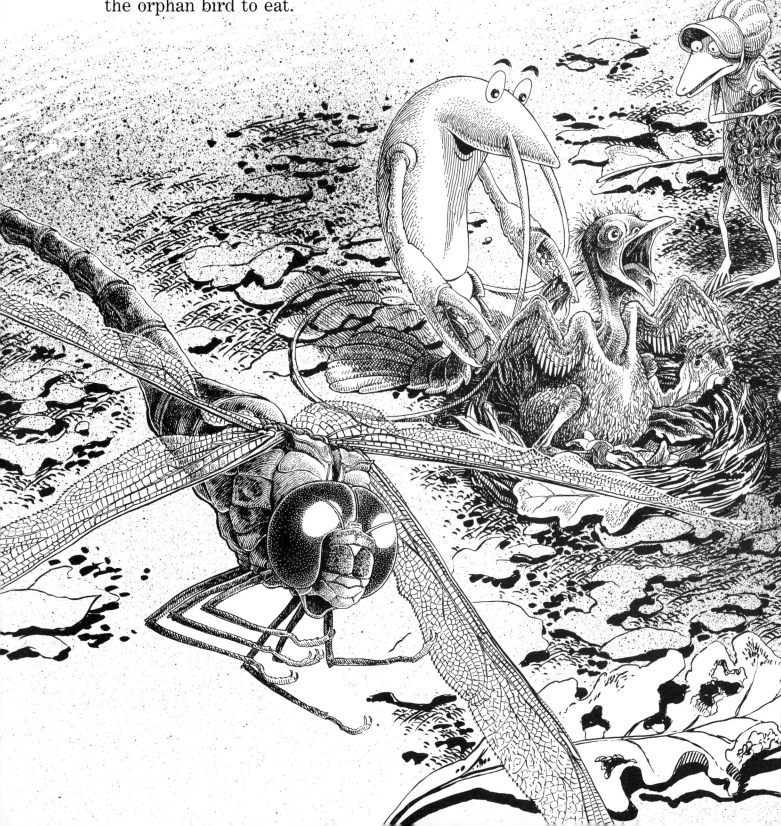

Christophe Cricket and Gaston Grasshopper were afraid to get too
close. So they sat on a limb of the live-oak tree and sang a lullaby:

Ferme tes yeux, p'tit Zo-Zo, fais do-do, fais do-do.
C'est tant mieux, p'tit Zo-Zo, fais do-do, fais do-do.
Tu n'a pas d' berceau, qui balance en haut,
Fais do-do, fais do-do, p'tit Zo-Zo.

Zo-Zo snuggled down in the warm grass. He tucked his head under
his wing and went to sleep.

Fais Do-Do, P'tit Zo-Zo

Words and music by Mary Alice Fontenot
Arranged by Joanna A. Pruitt

Ferme tes yeux, p'tit Zo- -Zo, fais do - - do, fais do- -do. C'est tant

mieux, p'tit Zo- -Zo, fais do- -do, fais do- -do. Tu n'a pas d' ber-ceau, qui ba-

lance en haut, Fais do- -do, fais do- -do, p'tit Zo- -Zo.

Translation for lullaby:

Close your eyes, little bird, go to sleep, go to sleep.
It is best, little bird, go to sleep, go to sleep.
You have no cradle to swing up high,
Go to sleep, go to sleep, little bird.

The next morning Zo-Zo woke up and began to chirp. His chirping got so loud that Clovis Crawfish came crawling, Maurice Mosquito Hawk came flying, and Fernand Frog came croaking.

"*Quoi y'a? Quoi y'a?*" croaked Fernand, which means "What's the matter?" in Cajun-French.

"Look!" said Clovis. "His mouth is wide open! His wings are fluttering! He must be hungry again! Hurry, get more food!"

Maurice Mosquito Hawk flew off to find more mosquitoes. Fernand Frog brought more fish eggs and Lizette Lizard dragged in some dried seeds.

All of Clovis Crawfish's friends brought something for the orphan bird to eat.

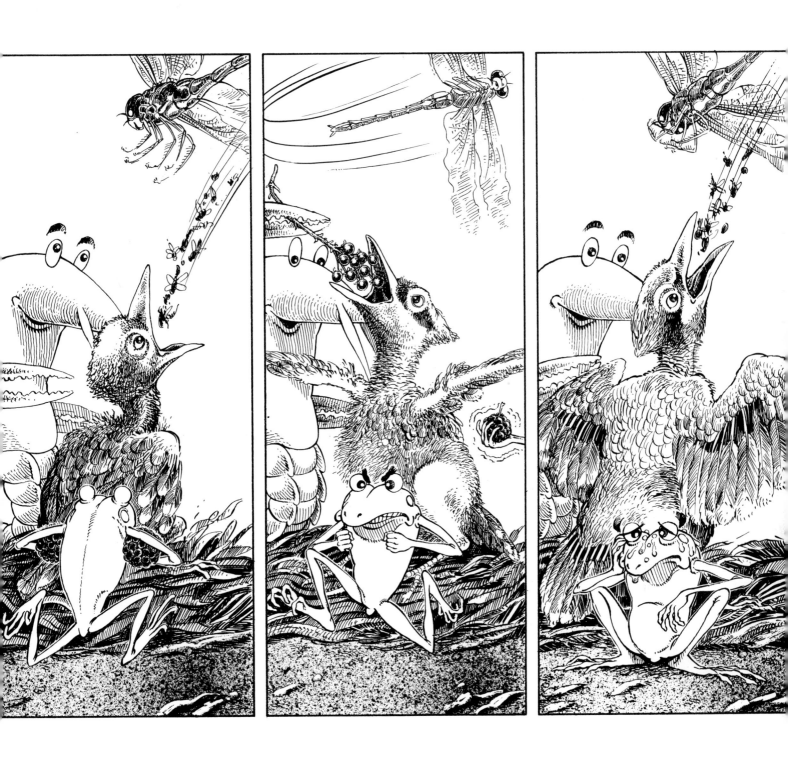

Zo-Zo grew fat and strong. His wing feathers grew out. Each night he snuggled down in the bed of warm grass while Christophe Cricket and Gaston Grasshopper sang him to sleep. Each morning he fluttered his wings and chirped and squawked until he got breakfast.

One day Lizette Lizard hauled in a ripe blackberry. Zo-Zo ate the berry, then grabbed Lizette by the tail. Lizette squealed; she twisted and wiggled and her tail broke off. She scurried up the muscadine vine and hid in the green leaves.

Clovis Crawfish flexed his claws and wiggled his whiskers fast, fast.

"*Maudit! Canaille!*" said Clovis, which means "naughty, naughty" in French.

"*Quoi y'a? Quoi y'a?*" asked Fernand Frog.

"That bird is big enough to feed itself!" said Clovis. "He just ate Lizette's tail!"

"What will Lizette do without a tail?" asked Fernand Frog.

"Oh, it will grow back," said Clovis. "But now that Zo-Zo can find his own food he'll have to go—before he tries to eat my other friends!"

"But Zo-Zo can't fly!" said René Rainfrog.

"Maybe he can," said Clovis. "Maybe he doesn't know he can fly! Let's find out!"

Clovis crawled over to Zo-Zo. He opened up his big sharp claws and pinched Zo-Zo's newly sprouted tail feathers, hard, hard.

"Chank! Chank!" squawked Zo-Zo. He fluttered his wings real fast and flew right up onto a branch of the live-oak tree.

Zo-Zo looked down and saw Clovis with his big sharp claws raised up.

Zo-Zo spread his wings and flew across the bayou.

International
Phonetics Transcription

dépêche-toi	*de pes twa*
p'tit zo-zo	*p ti ʒo-ʒo*
mais jamais	*mɛ ʒa mɛ*
pauvre 'tite bête	*poːvr tit bɛːt*
arrête	*arɛt*
quoi y'a	*kwa ya*
maudit	*mo-di*
canaille	*ka naːj*
ferme	*fɛrm*
yeux	*jøː*
berceau	*berso*
balance	*ba lãːs*
haut	** o*

David J. Theriot
Kenneth Douet
Earline Buckley

Teacher Training Specialists
Bilingual Service Center
University of Southwestern Louisiana

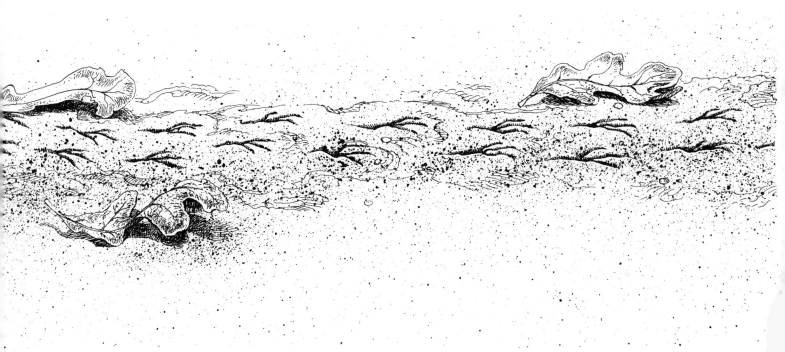